MY JOURNEY

SMALL TOWN, USA, CIRCA 1920-1930
OTHER RHYMES AND TYMES

DIECY LAWRENCE

Greenville, S.C.
2016

ISBN: 978-0-9725197-4-8

Requests for permission should be addressed to:

Fiction Addiction Publishing Services
1175 Woods Crossing Rd., #5
Greenville, S.C. 29607
864-675-0540
www.fiction-addiction.com
www.fpspublishing.com

Printed in the United States of America

Images and photos throughout are courtesy of the author, created by FPS, or drawn from photographs and images in the public domain.

ACKNOWLEDGMENTS

This book would never have materialized if my granddaughter, Beth Gallant, had not taken "the bull by the horns" and proceeded to do all the work necessary to get it published. Thank You, Beth!

I would also like to thank Judge Kendall Few, his wife Judith, and his assistant Phyllis Bowles for their invaluable help. They shared their knowledge to answer my many questions with valuable information.

Thanks to my great friends who read many of my poems and complemented my work. They were truly amazed to learn about the Great Depression from someone who lived through it.

I must also thank my family for their support, help, encouragement, and listening to recently written poems during our Sunday night dinners. I have three children, plus one deceased son, nine grandchildren, and nine great-grandchildren. They are a wonderful bunch and I am proud of each one.

To my son, Chip Gray: Thank you for all of the editing. Great job, "Chip"— a thousand thanks for your excellent suggestions. Thank you, Jacquelyn Vick, my daughter, for your support and encouragement. Thank you Phillip Gray, my #3 son, for your faithfulness through thick and thin.

I also want to thank all of my friends and associates who have provided the inspiration for my poems. My life is richer for having known you.

I have great memories of my grandparents, Mr. and Mrs. Enoch Lawrence who raised me. They would sit with me in front of an open fireplace, telling me stories about the history of this great country during the 1800's and early 20th century. They shared stories particularly of their lives during the civil war. These true stories I used as inspiration on many of my poems.

MY JOURNEY

SMALL TOWN, USA, CIRCA 1920-1930

OTHER RHYMES AND TYMES

CHAPTER I

SMALL TOWN, USA

I'd like to tell you about some of the people I relished

Some stories are true

Some are not

But all are embellished!

D. Lawrence

SMALL TOWN, U.S.A. Circa 1920's and 1930's

My town is tiny, located on the rolling hills of the Piedmont
Shady streets and a view of the Blue Ridge Mountains make it a beautiful spot
Things are very tranquil and excitement is rare
But what you hear makes up for the difference there
The place is full of characters, good and bad, bold and shy
The guys hang out on the corner and watch the girls go by.
The girls stroll along, flirt, and give the boys the eye.
A bunch of moochers saunter along the railroad track,
And no matter where they go, they always come back.
There's not much else to do in a town so small
A hot dog stand, drugstore, and depot don't make a mall
But no matter where I roam, this will always be home
So to it and the people there, I dedicate this poem.

THINGS REMEMBERED ~ 1920's

On Main Street stood the Amuzu picture show
  With a life sized poster of Clara Bow,
The very first "IT" girl,
Wearing a pleated skirt that exposed her legs
when she'd twirl
  Sixteen cents paid for popcorn, a coke and
admission;
A self-player piano furnished music
  During intermission
Talkies shook the nation like an explosion,
  Introduced by a resounding rendition
Of "Mammie" by Al Jolson
  Ruby Keeler and Dick Powell were a
Nimble dancing duo;
Tom Mix with his horse,
  Was the cowboy's hero.
The advent of radios and washing machines
  Changed the home scenes.

Telephones were something everyone wanted to try
  And Aeroplanes were seen in the sky.
Lindbergh astonished the world when he flew
  Over the Ocean blue
Industries, factories, and businesses were flourishing
  There was money and food for the perishing.
Things were happening so fast,
  The difference between fact and fantasy was hard to grasp
A good time was had by all,
  Nobody was prepared for the coming fall
These years are remembered with appreciation
  For all the good things they gave to our nation.

THE NEW FORD

In the late 1920's or early 1930's
  Rising like a star
Was the new Ford car
A Shiny four door sedan
A coupe with a rumble seat
Oh! They were neat!
Stick shift gears and automatic starter
Nothing could be smarter!
Everybody wanted one without a doubt
They cost $300.00 and nobody had that amount
Nobody had heard of an entrepreneur
But there was one for sure
Who developed a way to pay
That changed buying power across the land
Pay $25.00 a month for 12 months was the plan.
It brought customers in
  And that's how the great installment plan began

MR. FLETCHER GOLIGHTLY

Once a dear man named Mr. Fletcher
Decided to catch a train going to D.C.
So he could see the famous cherry trees
   blooming there
The cost was five dollars, and he had his fare
This was a time when few people had five dollars to spend

Friends and townspeople gathered at the station,
Plus the whole Golightly generation
Excitement filled the air —
The train would soon be there!
They heard the whistle blow
As the train pulled into the depot.
The brakes squeaked,
The train stopped,
The doors opened — The steps dropped
"All Aboard!" yelled the porter
"Bon Voyage!" was now in order

The Cherry Blossom Special sped along
Leaving behind a cheering throng
The thrill of a lifetime, you could tell
Three days and two nights in the nation's capital
A short visit to an earthly paradise: Truly a dream realized
There was never a happier event, in my recollection,
Than when Mr. Fletcher went to D.C. during the great Depression.

THE PREACHER WOMAN

There was a preacher woman who blew into town
 Riding in a white Chevrolet convertible, with the top down
She hit the town with a blast:
 The old sages said she wouldn't last.

She built a tabernacle on top of a hill,
 And on every meeting night the place would fill.
She preached to reach the souls she wanted to save
 From a life of sin and a fiery grave.

There was a man in the congregation
 Who was repentant, and responded to her invitation.
He was called Bubba, and he was a ladies' man
 Who ran a grocery store and a fruit stand

Short in stature, and not good looking in any respect,
 He could spot a pretty woman in just a sec.
Sister Thelma was a looker, young and spry
 And she immediately caught Bubba's eye.

Things were going great all the while,
 And Sister Thelma wore a great big smile.
She didn't believe anything could go wrong;
 The ministry had been successful for so long!

She was honored and loved by her congregation,
 Bubba more than anyone showed his appreciation.
Spirits were soaring, the money pouring in
 Satan couldn't stand it, so he brought in some sin.

The preacher woman and Bubba had gotten mighty tight
 And some folks didn't think it was right.
One night while they were praying with no light
 A woman slipped into the seat on Bubba's right.

As Sister Thelma prayed,
Bubba's hands strayed.
When the lights came on, Bubba's hands were black —
The woman had put soot on her legs — front and back.

The culprits were caught on the spot,
 And Bubba and the preacher woman were told to go where it's hot.
The old tabernacle is still standing there —
 A sinister reminder of the preacher woman's and Bubba's torrid affair.

MILKING THE COW

Milking the Cow.
  I never learned how
My cow would go dry
  No matter how hard I'd try
That cow wouldn't give as much
  When she felt my touch
She would shudder
  When I squeezed her utter.
That cow was nobody's fool
  Seeing me sit on that three legged stool
She kicked and swished her tail
  Until she turned over the milk pail.
And she probably laughed
  Because she knew I faced somebody's wrath
I hated that cow
  "Meow, Meow," the cat said
    Perched overhead
      Voicing her displeasure
        Over not getting her measure

SHOOTIN' UP THE TOWN

There was a shootout in Small Town, USA
I want to tell you about that infamous day.
One Sunday Morn a trio of religious fanatics
Decided they were sent from God to pull their antics.
Right in the middle of town by the drug store
In a Model T Ford they had guns and ammunition all over the floor
Two men and a woman jumped out wild eyed and ready to fire
On anybody and everybody who whetted their ire.
They were spewing fire and brimstone
Threatening all sinners who would not succumb
To their cult's beliefs and began to shoot in every direction
The poor church folks on their way home had to run for protection

They were shooting singing and shouting
It really was a fearful Sunday outing.
The police finally arrived and a standoff ensued
After a terrifying struggle they were finally subdued
Luckily they were poor shots so no one died.
Finally they were taken to the county jail with their feet and hands tied.

ODE TO TROTTIN' SALLY

Running along the train track
Stopping at every house and shack
Up the hill and through the valley
Everybody knew it was Trottin' Sally
Marked by a dog so his mama said
So he would never be right in his head
Running for miles with fiddle under his arm
Barking like a dog and causing alarm
With high steps and fiddle under his chin
His amazing antics would begin
A master of his fiddle and bow
He could put on quite a show.
When the fiddle barked like a dog and
talked too
People in the country side couldn't believe
it was true.
The man who never talked welcomed most
anything
With dancing, prancing and making his
fiddle sing.
When the train whistle blew long and hard
He'd halt, bark like a dog and run from the
yard.
Everybody was sad to see him go
Where he went no one would ever know.

Now, when we hear the train whistle blow,
We know that he is running up another hill
And through another valley
We will never forget you
And we salute You, Trottin' Sally.

MY SIS

My Sis is the meanest girl I have ever seen
Her beau says she's good but I thinks she's mean
She sits before her dresser and primps and paints,
She powders her nose until she almost faints
She has perfume that cost dollars and dollars,
And she pours it all over her dresses and collars,
When she goes to town she buys dresses and shoes
When dad gets the bill he has the blues.
She goes and comes when she pleases
Why she doesn't even have to take medicine when she sneezes
My Sis, she sho' does strut
Pshaw—I think she's a nut.

THE MOTHERLESS CHILD

The Weeping and wailing of the motherless child—Lo
No one else knows the depth of the grief—No
Those muffled cries and hot steaming tears.
In some dark quiet spot filled with many fears
A little heart beating with longing for someone gone.
A feeling of knowing she has to battle it alone
All tied up with many heartaches inside
Somehow you wish it had been you who had died.
Wiping away the tears on the bottom of your dress
Folding little hands together so tightly they press
Against a tear stained face daring to look above
Hunting and seeking for her and the assurance of love
The heavens look so immense and so far away
You know that reunion is for another day.
Suddenly you know you're in a different world
Too young but transformed from child to girl
Knowing now that your heart may again feel that rapture
When through your own children this love you will recapture

THIS LITTLE GIRL

I watched her cross the river bridge slowly
 This little girl crippled, bent and lowly.
I asked God in some way to bless,
So that she could withstand life's stress
 And all the extra pain she would have to bear
 Help her have hope and never despair
This little girl crippled, bent and lowly.

 Her hair is penciled tresses hangs,
She is barefoot, snaggle-toothed, with shaggy bangs
Her bent and dwarfed body causes her no concern
She is now too young troubles to discern.
This little girl, crippled bent and lowly.

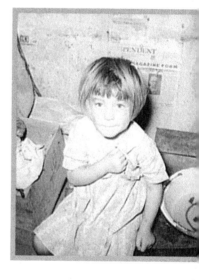

Love has been given her without stint
From a poverty stricken father who is also bent
Her mother is a simple soul who lends content
 To the dirty hovel and all the children sent.
Surrounded by a small world all her own
 Just a few acres and stream are all she's known
This Little girl crippled, bent and lowly.

When Father and Mother are gone and family torn apart,
 Will there be anyone to take this child into their heart?
When life becomes more serious than playing by the way
Dear God, please provide against that day
 For this little girl crippled, bent and lowly

IS THERE MOORE IN NEW YORK CITY?

There was a girl whose Dad was a mechanic for
  The Ford dealership in Moore.
She decided to seek her fortune in New York City;
  She wasn't talented, and she wasn't pretty
    She was shy, a tiny little thing
Who couldn't dance, and couldn't sing.
She went away, and against her father's will.
  She was tired of our little burg, and wanted a thrill.
He scraped a little money together, which wasn't much.
  Gave it to her, hugged her, and said "Keep in touch."
    The days and months passed, without a word.
She came home in a wooden box with the freight due.
His daughter was dead, how she died, he never knew.
I saw him many times, standing by the garage door,
But knew nothing of his heartache and burden he bore.

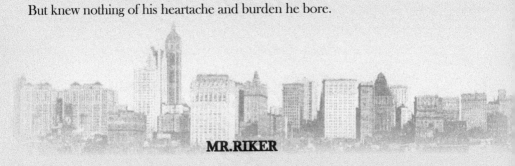

MR. RIKER

Every day Mr. Riker walked by our house
  On the dirt road, quiet as a mouse.
    No matter, rain or shine;
    He never seemed to mind.
  Through dust or mud with the same sad face,
His wife was "bad off" and he was a poor man;
His troubles were almost more than he could stand.
        As he passed.
      We always asked
"Mr. Riker, how is your wife today?"
"She's a little 'batter,' I believe!"
Then he'd wipe his nose on his sleeve.
We were puzzled: was she better, or worse?
We got our answer when we saw the hearse.

Dear Lord, please have mercy on Mr. Riker.

14

HUBERT

There was another fellow in my hometown that I want to bring to your attention.
 Hubert was good looking, and did some things I cannot mention,
But one day he pulled off the biggest act of all.
He climbed the water tank, big and tall.

It was located on a hill,
 Right next to the cotton mill
Where many people passed by,
 So he knew he would catch their eye.

While this is not an unusual feat,
 It caused a disturbance up and down our street.
There he was, his handsome body exposed,
 Because Hubert was inebriated, and forgot his clothes.

PANTS

We were told
 Of two women who were very bold.
They were wearing pants, what a disgrace!
 We jumped into our car and drove by their place.

There they were. We stared, entranced,
 Looking at two women in khaki pants!
Little did we know that this remarkable sight
 Would be the future women's delight!

PEG LEG JOHNSON

There was another person for whom I felt no pity;
Rumor was Peg Leg Johnson learned his evil ways in the big city
Everyone said he was the meanest man in town and had a leg of wood
What he did was so bad I never quite understood
    One day at school our teacher wanted lots
Of rich woods dirt for her flower pots.
    She sent a friend and me into the woods to see
If we could find just the right kind
We put our pots and shovels down
    And started digging in the ground
All of a sudden, who did we spy?
    But Peg Leg Johnson standing nearby
Seized with fear and terror we ran like kine
    Leaving our spades, pots, and dirt far behind
I can see him now, just as he stood
    With leering eyes there in the wood.

GUY

Guy was the man with the big head;
Tall thin, and always sad.
He owned a candy store across the street from the school
We were forbidden to cross the street, that was the rule.
So at recess, he'd cross over loaded with all kinds of treats
Peanuts, jaw breaker, suckers, and all kind of sweets
He'd count our pennies, nickels, and dimes
Glad to make a few cents in such hard times.
He'd tell us about the wife who'd left
And took all their money for herself.
All about their precious little child she took along
How lonely he'd been since they'd gone
Too proud to cry but couldn't hide his tears.
They never returned so poor Guy spent many lonely years.

ITS NONE OF YOUR BUSINESS

This fellow was an odd one indeed.
    He couldn't write and he couldn't read.
When he got a letter that he wanted read,
    He would stand behind the reader's head
And put a hand over each ear,
    So the reader couldn't hear
What the letter said.

CHAPTER 11

THE
GREAT DEPRESSION

P.S.

   I promised to continue the stories

   Of my town

So here goes the village bard

   And clown.

         D. Lawrence

THE GREAT DEPRESSION

I would be remiss to ignore the financial crash of 1929
And the Great Depression that followed right behind
It affected every citizen, child, woman, and man
A malaise of worry and fear covered the land
The poor became poorer groveling for a piece of bread,
Cold, ragged with no place to lay their head.
The wealthy became poor over night
They were in a pitiful plight
Most lost all their possessions and were dead broke
Some even lost their pride and died from suicide
The nation was awakened to a time of despair
There was no help anywhere.
In 1932 there was a glimmer of hope at last.
But recovery was no easy task.

HOBOS

Before the Great Depression "Hobos" were thought to be a sorry lot
But these hobos certainly were not.
They were a different breed;
A group of honorable men with a pressing need.
Jobs and prosperity were gone;
Their families were starving —
They could no longer hold on.
So they left them behind while they went to look for work of any kind.
Penniless, they hit the rails
And walked dusty trails.
They trudged along in despair,
Trying not to lose hope,
Saying another prayer.
Tearfully they knocked on doors along the way
Asking for bread because they had not eaten that day.
There were good people who sympathized with their plight;
They fed them, and let them sleep in the barn overnight
Hobos offered to do the most menial tasks to repay
Those who helped them along their way.
Upon leaving, they marked the mailbox posts
Belonging to their helpful hosts
So the next hungry fellow could find
Folks willing to help and who were kind.
What happened to those men?
They held on to the end.

SHANTY TOWN

Shanty town was something that I saw at a distance
My granddaddy took me by after much insistence
It was located behind the Chinaberry trees and the privet hedge
Between that and the river's edge
Shacks were built out of scrap lumber
Rusty tin and cardboard boxes.
In rags with bare feet the children ran around like little foxes
Small fires were burning in some spots
With tin cans used for cooking pots
Occasionally the children wandered "outside"
Bedraggled with bulging bellies and eyes open wide
Sure signs of pellagra, a disease rampant during the Depression
Caused by the neglect, hunger, and malnutrition
The hardships of this trying time
Plus this disease caused many people to lose their minds
An astounding fact, bums and beggars were not the main residents
The occupants were good folks ranging from farmers, factory workers,
    and bank presidents
People down on their luck through no fault of their own
Looking for any kind of work, just a job and a home.
No money, no food, no place to live, no possessions
All because of the Great Depression
Many people, especially the children, never survived
All were scarred by suffering before help arrived
It broke my heart to see their cruel fate
Realizing that help came too late
To my heart came the cry
"Except for the grace of God, there go I."

TURNING THE TIDES

Seared on my mind is the Great Depression
A time of hardship, despair and oppression
People were tired and worn,
 Broke, heart broken and forlorn.
Thin, pale children with bare feet
Were cold and had little to eat.
No jobs, no money caused parents to be worse
All suffering from the depression's curse.
"5 cent cotton, 40 cent meat. How in the world could a poor man eat?"
Eventually the cotton fields with bole weevils were gone
Even the wealthy were stripped to the bone

But somehow hope never died
With courage and pride the people did decide
That they would overcome the misery and that changed history
There were great promises that fueled the fire in 1932
By a new president who believed and he knew what to do.
The Great new day, the new deal, the job corps and the WPA
During that decade the people made
Great strides
That turned the Tides
Which helped lay the
foundation of the world's
greatest Nation.

REVERE

I look out my window in despair
And see God's wondrous garden there
No matter the day or hour
No matter sun or shower
Night or Day
It never goes away
The beauty gives repose
Peace comes from the rose
I sit in my chair
The loving spirit of God is there
I bow my head in prayer
Lift my voice in praise
For His faithfulness
Today and always.

THE 50th REUNION

In the days before pantyhose, instant pudding, microwaves and television
A couple of men who wanted to rule the world made a decision
To start a terrible war that was raging in 1943
When a group of young ladies whose loved ones were in the military
Gathered together in the First Baptist Church sanctuary

That's how the Deborah class was born
Fifty years ago on one Sunday Morn.
We joined together to study God's word
To offer prayers that we know were heard
Loving support in gladness, sorrow and tears
Have been shared among us during those years.
There were some sad days when news was not good for our side
There was heartbreak, friends and loved ones died.
Peace came at last and there was joy in the land.
Families were reunited and changes were made in our little band
Some left us for opportunities in other places
Others came and we welcomed those new faces.
The next few years were spent wiping noses and changing diapers
Then came the time of Barbie Dolls, Indian whoops, and cowboy snipers.
There have been graduations, weddings and grandchildren galore
Fourth of July celebrations, picnics, Christmas, Easter and much more

Only God knows why some are blessed with children
And some are blessed in other ways
But regardless, He has enough for us to do to fill our days

Our hearts have been broken and opened wide
When our loved ones have slipped away to the other side
God bless us all, through thick and thin we've clung
Representing the finest and very best women in God's kingdom

When it comes to teachers we have been richly blessed
Those dear, wonderful women were and are God's absolute best,
Enriched our souls and taught us how to serve the Lord
We are eternally grateful and great will be their reward
Now here we sit with our aches and pains
Our memories gone never to return again
We've lost a lot of our of our hair and a lot of our teeth
Our faces are lined with dark blotches underneath
How much wisdom did our weary heads bring?
We don't know where we are going or where we've been
We look at one another and it's very plain
That it's hard for us to remember the others' names
It's been a wonderful fifty years, yes indeed!
There have been years in which God has met our every need
He has kept us and blessed us beyond measure
His love and mercy are things we treasure
Through all life's way he has been most gracious
And He has prepared for us a heavenly home most spacious
In the meantime we still have things to do
So let's praise the Lord and worship Him until life is through.

MARY LILLIE

Our childhood days on Howard Street...
The summers we ran up and down the street with bare feet,
The dust so deep it squished between our toes,
Bubbled up and stained our clothes,

Roller skating for hours,
Picking May flowers,
Those flower baskets for May Day,
How we put them on porches, and then ran away;

Coming home from outings in the dark of night,
Together we ran, gripped with fright,
Racing by the drug store, the lumberyard, the gin,
Trembling as we passed a place known for sin;

Picking cotton, breaking our backs,
Trudging home in the evening, dragging our sacks.
A penny a pound is what we made
After all the cotton was weighed.

We saved every penny, nickel, and dime
So we'd have money when it came fair time.
The county fair was an exciting event —
We went, and we laughed, and we spent every cent.

Food, daring rides, side shows all about...
To this day, I can still hear the barker shout:
"Hot dogs! Hot dogs! Wiener in the middle, pickle on top!
Makes your lips go flippity flop!"
One year I had an awful fate —
The car door came off when I hit the gate!
All my hard-earned money was gone
After I paid for putting it back on.

We never made
"The Hit Parade,"
A favorite show
On the radio.
But "Laugh, Clown, Laugh" was our favorite song -
You played the piano, and I sang along.

Those were memorable rides to Rainbow Lake
In that four-door Chrysler model 1928.
Traveling those country roads, we felt safe then;
For everyone who came along was our friend.
It was so much fun on a hot summer day
To jump in that icy cold water and play.

Those were glorious days when snow closed our school!
We rode on a homemade sled, pulled by an old mule.
We made snow men, and slipped and slid around
Threw snowballs, and finally hit the ground.

Remember "Burvee," your brothers' nurse?
I was so sorry for her, and never felt worse
Than when we got the garden rake
And forced her to kill that scary snake.

In the deepest Depression, do you recall?
How we ran all over town,
Contacting everybody around?
Because you wanted to win a contest,
So you were doing your very best
To sell subscriptions to the daily news
Even though most folks couldn't pay the dues.

You wouldn't believe it,
And were determined to achieve it.
We were all excited and had conniptions
When you won for selling the most subscriptions!
We were ecstatic when we realized
A trip to the World's Fair in New York was your prize!

When being grown up seemed so far away?
All the dreams we had about "someday"?
Like,
Having our own car?
Becoming a movie star?
Being a beauty queen,
Just like in the movie magazine?
Going to exotic places,
Having beautiful bodies and faces?
Marrying a rich, handsome man?
Living happily for a long life span?
How many children would there be -
One, or two, or maybe three?
Those were just the teenaged years;
We were consumed with curiosity and fears.
There were many questions we didn't dare ask,
Because we had heard about girls with a "past."

Childhood and adolescence ends;
Too quickly adulthood begins.
We lose contact with old friends,
But memories remain;
And we wish we could live those days again.

CHAPTER III
RHYMES & TIMES

P.S.

  This is a little note

About these poems I wrote

To help you put bad memories

  On the shelf

And laugh at yourself!

        D. Lawrence

OLD POETS NEVER DIE, THEY JUST SIMMER

Hello, is this the end of the line
When I find
I'm exhausted and dead tired
Rhyme less and uninspired?
As I try to get my lines together
My head seems light as a feather   Oh!
Feather—that's a good word—let's see
        "Feather bed"
I'm going to hunt one and lay down my head.
What do I dream? Well, it's my guess
I'm in the middle of a chicken's nest.
I hear the cackling hen and crowing rooster
And little dibbies peeping, just like they useter.
I've got to get out of here, and in a hurry!
Get moving! Here comes something big and furry!

Horns and saddle bags make a terrible sight
I scurry and escape into the black of night
Only to discover my same old desperate self -
Am I an old worn out poet who's been put on the shelf?
Indeed not, it's the summer heat -
I'm going where it's cool, and put up my feet.
Within my being, the storm clouds roll,
Waking my body and renewing my soul.
All clouds have a silver lining, please remember
And old poets never die - they just simmer.
So you've not read my last line yet -
Someday I'll write a poem you'll never forget.

Oh, the sweet essence of the gentle rain
 Watering the parched earth with sweet refrain
Of musical drops
 Renewing, reviving our grassland and crops.
Listening with reverence and rejoicing
To the steady beat of rhythmic voicing.
 Played upon the thirsty soil and flowers
As time passes, minutes and hours
 Thankful for each silver, wet globule
 Falling, falling in the fresh air so cool.
For this we have waited, for this we have prayed.
 Oh, the blessing of God has never betrayed,
He opens the heavens in his own time
 And sends the showers sublime.

A DUMMY"S COMPUTER GLOSSARY

I am one of those poor souls who is computer illiterate
   Training is available and I do consider it
I'm going to enter the next class
   So at last
I won't be considered a dolt
   Even though I'm oldt
Because of this method of communication
   I'm in an embarrassing situation
The glossary is completely lost on me
   The crazy terminology
Sounds like mythology
   Instead of being a horrible creature
The "mouse" is now a respectable feature.
   There are no spiders that "byte"
When caught up in the "web-site"
   A "virus" does not cause a cold in the head
It messes up the whole computer instead.
   A "boot" has nothing to do with shoes.
"Multimedia" has no interest in the news.
   Did you know your "e-mail" won't get wet?
When you surf the "internet."
There is something odd about the "Chat-room"
Not a word is said, it's as silent as a tomb.
   A "hack" isn't what it used to be.
Now it's a nerd you never see.
"Hard drive" no longer applies to an automobile.
   "Software" has no feminine appeal.
"On line" sounds like being hung out to dry.
   And something else I decry.
How do you "get in" when you never been out?
What's "being down" all about?
Are "ROM" and "RAM" twins?
   Are icons really pretends?

"Set up wizard" is not from Oz.
  And "illegal gibberish" is not becuz, because.
The "recycling center" doesn't take tin cans
  "Floppy discs" aren't held together with rubber bands
"Mode" I love pie-a-la mode, don't you?
  Well, that meaning will never do.
There are two other things most incredible
  Not a drop to drink can be had in the "bars."
And there's nothing on the menu that's edible.
  How do you open a dialog box?
How do you get "dry bones" out of windows that are locked?
  "Dot" was a charmer and friend until the day
When "Com" spirited her away.
  So many strange words and terms.
It's just like opening a can of worms.
  There's just one word that expresses my frustration
I don't know what it means but it is spelled "OBFUSCATION."
  After that, I'd "beta" button my mouth and hide my face.
Open a window and fly into cyber space.

THE OWL AND THE HONEY BEE

The wise old owl and the little honey bee
  Had their homes in the same old tree.
None were ever so different as these two,
The honey bee buzzed, and the owl said, "Who?"
One evening the bee buzzed around the owl's head.
  The owl sat quietly. "Who?" was all he said.
  Agitated, the bee asked, "Is that all you can do?
Perch high on a limb, and at night ask who?"
  I can make honey, I can buzz, and I can sting
  Altogether, I'm a pretty powerful thing.
With those big eyes rolling round and round,
  All you can do is make one sound.
  "If you're as wise as they say,

Why do you stay awake all night and sleep all day?
  What goes on in those dark hours?
I prefer daylight, and sunshine, and flowers.
  Since we're as different as night and day,
  I'd like to hear what you have to say!"
   The wise old owl replied,
  As he opened his eyes very wide,
"You talk so big, and you are so little-
  In that I find a puzzling riddle.
But that has little effect on the scheme of things
"We have little in common, but we both have wings.
  Why can't we be who we are, and agree
 That I' m an owl, and you're a honey bee?
  So let us be who we are
And do the things we were created for."
  Day turns to night,
  The bee ends his flight.
   The tree bends.
The stars shine all night long
Day breaks, and there's a new dawn.

I'VE ALWAYS WANTED TO WIN A CONTEST

I've always wanted to win a contest
No doubt, my entries have been the best!
I'm talented with words and phrases,
I'm clever at working puzzles and mazes,
My jingles never fail to rhyme -
I fill in every space and line,
Dot every "I" and cross every "T",
Have a perfect solution for every mystery.
Stay up late, get up early.
Become bleary-eyed and surly.
Can't eat breakfast, lunch, or dinner;
Somehow I know I have a winner.
Rush to the post office, all in a heat,
Because there is a deadline to beat.
The waiting begins, until that fateful day
When a voice on the phone will speak up and say,
"You're a winner!"
"A Jaguar?"
"No."
"A Cruise?"
"No."
"Well, What?"
Dead silence.
"Sorry. This is a wrong number I've got."

PUZZLED

Is your mind filled with wonder and doubt?
Are you puzzled at what this world is about?

Do questions fill your head?
Do Answers cause you to feel misled?
Join the millions who have inquiring minds?
Who travel life's highways with no road signs?

Why do some people have good health and some bad?
  Why are some happy, while others are sad?
    Why are some burdened with many cares?
    While others enjoy life's finest fares.
Why are some good and others bad?
  What other choices have they had?
Why are some homely and others handsome?
Why are some poor, and others have a king's ransom?
    What about different races,
    With different skin color and faces?
What about mysterious places and faraway lands?
What about glaciers, oceans, mountain tops and desert sands?
What about the moon, the sun, the stars?
  Do people live on Venus, Pluto and Mars?

We could ask questions like this until doomsday:
We could consult with seers and scientists to hear what
they say.
      Each opinion would vary to such a degree
    That our minds would react with a great melee.
We never will know how or why,
No matter how hard we try!
We strive to live, and yet won't have the answers when we die.
We must put our trust in the One who does know
And live our lives in love, peace, and compassion show.

LATE TO BED, LATE TO RISE

Late to bed and late to rise,
  The sweetest sleep is after sunrise.
At nighttime with vacuum and mop
  I clean my house from bottom to top.
Tis my family's delight
  To eat the cakes I bake at night.
My family's rips and tears, maybe a hem torn,
  All are repaired and ready for them by morn.
Dinner guests who stay after nine
  Are no problem. I'll get to work on time.
Late church suits me best,
  By that time I'm ready and dressed
To wake with sunbeams streaming in my window
  And dew drops glistening below
Get me moving in a trot,
  Dragging around half asleep I'm not.
My biological clock follows a different drummer
  But just because I'm a late person doesn't make me any dumber.

Now that I'm older and my family is gone,
  I'm still a late person but the drummer is playing a different song.

RETIREMENT

I need your patience during my dotage
I'm going strong but there is a shortage
  In my voltage.
No longer am I up at the crack of dawn.
Now I wake up roll over stretch and yawn,
  Fall back to sleep with not a thought
About property being sold and bought.
  Retirement is something we all anticipate,
But it's not the same when we participate.
  "You need to rest and play."
  So they say.
But, Oh my, how I miss my pay day.

THE BOOK CLUB

The Athenaeum Book Club, what a proper name
 For a group of very proper ladies, whose aim
Is to enrich their lives by reading the latest books in print,
 Books gathered together, and each month to the members lent.

To be read and returned for the next member's pleasure,
 For the joy of reading during her hours of leisure.
Pages full of wonderful things, surprises, and mysteries so intense.
Floating on gossamer wings into the land of make believe and suspense.

Reaching into the deepest secrets of heart and soul
 Bringing back dreams never forgotten, never told.
Ah, what joy is a good book, a very dear friend
 That we hate to leave before we reach the end.

So our very proper book club is just what it should be --
 Friendship, fellowship, sharing our books while sipping a cup of tea.

THIRTEEN

Giggling, laughing, having so much fun
 There's no time to get homework done.
Thirteen is certainly a magical age.
 As Shakespeare said, "all the world's a stage."
Thirteen-year-olds never come in ones,
 There are always more than two
And giggling is their favorite thing to do.
 Giggling at the dinner table, giggling in bed.
Giggling at everything that's said.

Life is so topsy turvy and such a delight
 When one can giggle at everything in sight.
Giggling about brother, sister, dad and mother
 Or just giggling about each other.
A giggle or a wiggle can start it up again
 There's no rhyme, reason or plan.
Laughing faces, giggling sounds simply abound
 And make hearts sing.
When you're thirteen and all around
 Are such funny giggly things.

A GHOST OR NOT!

Do you believe in ghost, neither do I
    But I can't deny
That on an eerie moonlit night
 Something happened to excite
 A couple of friends and me,
 As We
Were chugging toward
Home In that 1935 Ford.
    Dreamily cruising up route 176
Two guys and a girl were an unusual mix,
    But life was sweet as we drifted along,
Love and romance were great and life was a song.
 The music on the radio
 Was playing very low.
As we passed a graveyard going slow.
 Everything was quiet and serene
When a man and a boy came on the scene
 Walking hand in hand on the right of way,
        The night was cool,
     The moon was bright as day,
     Their images were perfectly clear.
A man and a little boy as we drew near.
    We could see them so well
    That we could tell
The roly-poly man wore suspenders and was
About 30 or so, short and stout.
 The child was chubby, about three or four
 They were there, then they were gone!
     Never to be seen anymore.
A swirling vapor rose from the ground.
 There was silence, dead silence, not a sound.
     We were stunned and speechless until
     The old Ford sputtered going up a hill.
That sputter caused us to shutter.
 And stare at each other.
Very timidly one of us asked
 "Did you see something peculiar?
 As we passed?"
 To this day none of us know what we saw
Or didn't see
 To us it is still a mystery
Now your opinion I petition
Was it a ghost or an apparition?

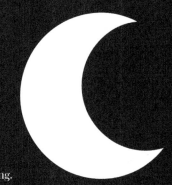

HER MAJESTY THE NIGHT

When the sovereign sun sets at the end of the day
  Her Majesty the night appears in regal array
Her raiment is adorned by the sparkling stars
  The beauty of Venus, the glowing embers of Mars.

Never was the world so lovely as by moonlight
  Never so peaceful as when cradled by her Majesty the night.
Never was man so shorn of pride and pretense
  As when meditating in her tranquil presence.

Many who have been forced into flight
  Are hidden in the cloak of her majesty the night.
Honored by a tiny babe whose father had to flee
  With him under his cloak to Egypt from Bethlehem

Her stars are guideposts and her moon lights the way
  For many weary travelers who have become lost during the day
Many Vessels off their course have been set aright
  By the ever helping hand of her majesty the night.

She sprinkles star dust on the young at heart
  As under her sparkling sky romance gets its start
Her starlight ignites the spark of true love
  As she blesses it with moon beams from above

The beauty is admired by the sentry at his post
  Her glory has been proclaimed by the heavenly host
Ever so majestic her splendor is the poets delight
  None can rival, none can compete with her majesty the night.

GRANDPA AND ME

During my first childhood it was expected that all children be good
A Motherless child at 18 months
At age 15, on a cold miserable day
My grandmother passed away

Now my grandpa and I were on our own
I drove that 1930 Chevrolet over hills and plains
And down pasture lanes
No matter the snow over the slick roads we'd go

A box of ashes, a tow sack and a shovel in the back
Very handy if we got stuck in all that muck
Grandpa and his buddies
Sang the music of shaped notes
That author singing Bill Weaver wrote
When the tuning fork gives the pitch they
Sing acapella without a hitch

The years that passed in between seem like a dream
My second childhood arrived too fast.
Now I'm wondering "How long will it last?"

MEMORIES

BOO HOO

I have a short circuit in my brain
  I can't remember your name.
Humiliated? Yes, but what can I do
  Those names just won't come through

Some folks don't understand my condition
  Are puzzled by my brain's attrition
I can remember when Lindbergh flew the ocean blue
  And tell you who won the presidential election of 1932

I can recite names of yesterday's movie
  Stars by the score
But I can't tell you the name
  Of the guy next door.

I can bore you stiff talking
  About the Great Depression
Bread lines, the cold, the unemployed
  With their gaunt expression.

Then came FDR to save us
  With the New Deal and the WPA
The promise of a better tomorrow
  And a great new day.

The horror of World War II is still
  Vivid in my mind
The last great war, so it was said,
  For all mankind.

Why do I remember so much
  From the days of yore
And can't remember what I went for
  When I get to the store?

My friends, when I meet you
  And look you in the eye
I'll give you my warmest smile
  But am about to cry

It's a pitiful plight
  And isn't it a shame
That I can't recall
  My best friend's name.

STORY OF A SOUTHERN REDNECK

I visited a northern city in the days of yore
  Being Southern to the core
I decided to visit a church there
  I entered the church just before the Morning Prayer
There was an attentive congregation
  A wonderful example of integration
When the collection plate was passed and
  A song was sung
  The preacher begun
Here is what the preacher said
  "Ladies and gentlemen this is black history month
    You know nothing about segregation, the oppression
    The suffering inflicted on black people
    Because you have lived in this great city
    And state. Now if you had lived with those
    Rednecks in South Carolina, Georgia, Alabama or Louisiana
    You would have a different history."
Holding onto my seat, I promised myself that if I got the chance
    I'll make that preacher dance.
When I exited into the vestibule there the preacher stood
  This was my chance to get him good.
I said, "Mr. Preacher, I'm a proud redneck from South Carolina."
He went ballistic and did a great dance!
  I held out my hand
And said "There are no hard feelings man."
  He finally quieted down!
I caught my flight and left town
  I had never thought about whether or not
I was a redneck before
  So I gave myself a test and here is the score
I passed! I made 100, Yes, Yes, Yes!
Here's the Test...
IF you call the noon meal dinner and the evening meal
Supper, you're a redneck.
IF you eat pinto beans and collard greens, you're a redneck
IF you take the letter S from the word "square," you're a redneck

Oh Well, what the heck.
I love being a "redneck"!

CHAPTER IV

SEASONS

P.S.

I'm going to stop here for tonight

But there are many more stories

I intend to write

Good Night!!

D. Lawrence

2000 YEAR JUBILEE

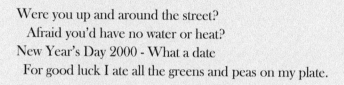

A New Year, a new century
  A new millennium
May your joys be megaton
  Your sorrows minimum
Thank goodness for an uneventful Y2K
    What happened to the doomsayers that day?

Were you up and around the street?
  Afraid you'd have no water or heat?
New Year's Day 2000 - What a date
  For good luck I ate all the greens and peas on my plate.

I never dreamed I'd live to celebrate
  A new century, a new millennium. But it's great
To anticipate all the technical advancements
  With the marvelous unimaginable enhancements
Not yet a figment of man's mind
  What will the century find?

To compare
  With the world's changing fare.
Success and riches bait us
  Fortune and fate await us

Many miracles seem to be in sight
  Not only in medicine, space, and flight
Conquering every fatal disease
  Painful and tormented minds at ease.

Overcoming deformity
  In its enormity
Life will be much longer
  Our bodies will be healthier and stronger
The promise of a great future surrounds us
  The question is. "Can we subdue our greed, hate and lust?"

Where will the homeless sleep
 What will the hungry eat?
What will the naked wear?
  Will there be justice anywhere?
What will erase the pain?
  Of suffering and shame?

What will heal the broken heart?
  What will give the failure a new start?
Will the golden rule be invoked?
  Until the hearts of men are woked.

To the need of love, mercy and caring
  For how our fellow man is faring
Until misery is wiped from the Earth
  And dignity given to every person birthed
All will be futile and to no avail
  Unless the love and mercy of God
Are allowed to prevail

I can't play the piano, I can't play an organ,
   and I can't sing
As a matter of fact, I can't do much of
   anything.
Though in my muddled mind sometimes
Words bunch together and make rhymes
Some are good, some are bad, some are
   funny, some are sad
I volunteered to read an Easter poem
But, alas my mind is so dense
The words won't make sense
Being utterly dismayed, I prayed:
"Dear Heavenly Father,
Please help this insignificant poet
Write a magnificent poem."
I listened but I never heard
Not even a word!
So in my despair
I wrote the poor poet's prayer:

"Heavenly Father,
I want so much to honor
   the life and the resurrection
Of your only son, Jesus Christ,
   at this Holy time,
So, please, give me profound
Thoughts and words that rhyme.
It is my deepest desire to convey
In words from heart and soul,
Feelings of joy, praise, and thankfulness
That from my inner being roll
I'm such a poor poet trying so hard
To write something sublime,
Worthy words and thoughts fail me;
They will not come from my unworthy mind
Oh Lord, you know my heart, my feeling,
love, praise and adoration
In awe and humility I bow down
Before the cross where Jesus suffered
And died for my salvation
Then dare I look and see the glorious sunrise
The empty tomb and hear the joyous cries
   Jesus has risen!
      Jesus has risen!
Hallelujah, Hallelujah, Hallelujah
Jesus Christ lives today!

VALENTINES

Valentines are for lovers, of that there's no doubt;
Hugs, Kisses, "I Love Yous" are what it's about.
   Dream the dream of a lover,
   And you'll soon discover
  Life will never be the same
   After Cupid takes his aim
   And strikes you in the heart
   With his searing magic dart.
Your whole being is in a whirl
It's a delightful, delicious world
  Full of kisses that taste like wine
   And hugs for your valentine.
   Red roses, boxes of candy in red;
That Valentine feeling really goes to your head!
  Sometimes jewels and other surprises appear
  Like exotic perfume, so fragrant and rare.
  Oh golly, oh gee! What a wonderful feeling
Hearts throbbing, knees knocking, send you reeling.
The whole generation is celebrating this wonderful time
So get in the mood, and grab your Valentine!

FOURTH OF JULY

It's time to join the celebration
　Of the birthday of our great nation
The first thing to do
　Is to hang out the red, white and blue.

In memory of those patriots who
　Paid the ultimate price
And in honor of those who defend it today

We are thankful that our homeland
　Turned out to be
The land of the brave
　And the home of the free.

Let's join the parade
　Listen to the speeches made
And the music played
The "Star Spangled Banner" and "America."

Salute the flag as our young people march by
　These fine young people represent
　People across our land
Who hold the future of this Nation
　In their hands.

Let's never forget the cost
　That was paid
The prayers that were said and
　The dreams that were made
By great men like Washington
　And women like Betsy Ross.

May they be the example for
　Honor, bravery and faith
That will guide the future
　And keep this land great.

God Bless America!

THANKSGIVING MEDITATION

A Little quiet time with God among the autumn leaves,
Of darkest green, bronze, red and gold-
Time to meditate, pray and renew my soul
How thankful I am that He found me here
Walking in the woods seeing His handiwork everywhere.
A Heart full of thanksgiving at this time of year
For all the beauty of the harvest time atmosphere
Caused me to pause and humbly thank Him
For filling the world with unsurpassable beauty
To the brim.

CHILDREN'S HALLOWEEN

Halloween, Oh Halloween, a time of Ghosts and Ghouls
Black magic, witches, clowns and flopped-eared mules.
Children masquerading, laughing, parading
Up and down the streets with sacks to collect their treats.

Gaily costumed kids by the score
Come knocking on my door
They are a delightful sight
And merriment fills the night
So precious - Cowboys, spacemen and a goblin
Skeletons, hobos, and Donald Duck a-wobbling
Little Bo Peep, an angel with wings
Lions, tigers and all kinds of scary things.

Firecrackers popping, noise makers never stopping
Children's squealing voices, loud and deafening noises
Candy, gum and a child's excited scream
This is fun! This is Hall-O-Ween!

SNOW

Silently, silently the big fluffy flakes fall
  Covering tree tops and garden wall
Rooftops with icy white frosting glisten
  A bird call pierces the air, the only sound, listen!
The world moves slowly and carefully along.
  As though heeding the bird's song
Seeking family, safety and warmth of home
  In his desire for these things he is not alone.
The bird calls again for the mate he has not found
  Calling, calling, echoing the plaintive sound
Ah, there is a quietness now, don't say a word
  Suddenly the silence is broken by a shrill from the bird
So like the bird is man, seeking and calling
  For loved ones when the snow is falling.
The beautiful, beautiful snow so white
  As it covers the earth, it comes from God
We know
  So white, so pure, just as our sins are washed clean
Covered in the blood of the lamb never more to be seen.
  Snow, blessed snow coming from above
A symbol of God's pure love,
As the swirling flakes come spiraling down
  The glory of God doth abound
And nestled underneath the window sill
  Sits the sparrow and his mate peaceful and still

CHRISTMAS **FRENZY**

I've got to hurry, I've got to go
Shop, shop, shop, go, go, go
I must check my list one more time.
I don't mind shopping but hate waiting in line
A Christmas tree, A Christmas tree
Standing there as bare as can be
It's got to be decorated ...decorated right away.

Presents to buy, cookies to bake, cards to address
Ribbons, papers, tinsel oh what a mess.
Mercy, the garland and lights are entangled
Dear Lord help me, my nerves are jangled.

Calm, Oh calm I always get it done.
It's really not hard and is a lot of fun
When I see the stockings hung in a row
And the Christmas tree all a glow

I get the wonderful Christmas spirit
And I know
It is all worthwhile
Because we are celebrating the birth
Of the Christ child

CHRISTMAS AFTERMATH

Father in his easy chair, nursing an "overstuffed pouch,"
  Mother is exhausted and is stretched out on the couch
The Christmas tree lights are signaling distress,
And the baby's on the floor, making more mess.

  The candles are teetering this way and that
The mistletoe is falling after being hit with a bat.
  The holly, once so red and green and bright
  Is entangled with a ribbon and looks a fright.

A Christmas radio is playing at top volume,
The house shakes as a firecracker hits a column.
Junior races through the house on his new tricycle
  As he passes, the poor tree drops another icicle.

  In the yard Cowboys and Indians give a war whoop,
The little girls grab their dolls and run for the stoop.
  The frightened dog dashed out of sight,
  The cat scampers after with all her might

  The clutter of toys and food strewn all over the place
  Would cause the trash man to hide his face.
  Inside and outside, everything looks a disgrace.
  Christmas- It's all over - yep! All over the place!

STROLLING DOWN THE BOULEVARD

I took a walk tonight, two nights before Christmas Eve
I felt I needed something and something I did receive
The magic of the night filled the air
The spirit of our Lord was everywhere

Rain drops glistened and lights flickered
Silhouetting trees against the sky
They shed a glorious light as darkness fell
And moonbeams floated by
Oh, Holy star, the fair weather star of that wondrous
    night
On all of us pours forth the mirage of love and light
Silent night, Holy night, rang that dear old hymn
As I fathomed the mystery and magic of that night in
    Bethlehem
The splendor of the night filled my soul as I strolled
    the Boulevard
My whole being responded with praise and love for my
    Lord
The magnificence of that night held me entranced
I, even I, Privileged to know God's only son, can claim
    the gift of the holy one

Raise our voices, let us sing and shout
And tell the world what it's all about
The King has come to Earth, Joy, Joy, Joy!
Mary's little boy.

THE FIRST CHRISTMAS

The trip to Bethlehem was
    long and dreary
Joseph and Mary, great with child, were
    tired and weary
A tax was due and they came to pay
But couldn't find a place to stay.
Finally the Inn keeper offered a stable

Mary delivered the Holy Child at the end of that day
And laid him in a trough filled with hay.
The angel of the Lord told Mary to name him Jesus,
God's gift of His only Son, The Holy One, to us.
Glory, Glory, the Angels sang
Announcing the birth of the New Born King.

On that cold winter night shepherds were watching their sheep
When suddenly they were awakened from their sleep.
When the angels' song they did hear
They trembled with fear.
The angel said, "Fear not. I bring you good tidings
Of great joy, which shall be to all people."
As soon as the angels and the Heavenly Host were gone,
They said to one another, "Let's go see this thing that is known."
God's great love and the star's bright light
Guided them through that night
Until they came to the place where Jesus lay
Asleep on the hay.
Glory, Glory to the new born King of the Earth, yea,
Whose Kingdom is here to stay.

This is the same Jesus who died on the cross and rose again
To save us from our sin,
Bringing peace on earth and good will to men.
Praise God in the highest
Let the bells ring
As all God's children praise their King.

Hallelujah, Hallelujah, the angels sing!
Amen, Amen

CHRISTMAS THEN

My, how Christmas really has changed over the years,
Thoughts of how Christmas was brings a few tears
To my eyes that are not quite as bright as they used to be:
My body is not as agile either, as you can plainly see.

One of the nice things about growing older is that
Others do all the rushing around,
Getting everything in order and shopping until the last present is found
As I look back, Mama and Papa made a wonderful Christmas for us:
But, it all seemed so easy with no strain or fuss

I can hear Papa now telling Mama as he came in the back door
"I got the fattest turkey in the coop. I'll take the others down to the store
I'll swap them for calico, peppermint sticks, and surprises galore.
We'll stack presents around the tree 'til they cover the floor."
At this moment, the excitement of Christmas began, but it was understood
That we had to be on our P's and Q's and had better be good.

Every Christmas Eve going into the pasture to
    get the tree was a great thrill
We ran down the lane and always picked the
    prettiest one at the top of the hill.
When we got home with the tree, Mama always
    met us at the kitchen door.
The sweetness of pumpkin and mince pies
    she'd cook never smelled so good before.
Decorating the Christmas tree was a time of
    sheer delight
We pulled and stretched in every direction
    trying to get everything placed just right
It's funny now, but surely wasn't that Christmas
    Eve long ago.

We were afraid we'd get switches in our stockings, because we
    were fighting so.
Our brothers, full of themselves, hid our popcorn ropes out in the
    barn.
The Mice found them before we did and nothing was left except
    the yarn.

Christmas morning came very early, long before daybreak
We tried to peek at the tree before Mama and Papa were awake
But we couldn't keep quiet, no matter how hard we tried
Soon everyone was at the tree impatient and wide-eyed.

Before a present was opened, before much was said,
Papa motioned for each one of us to bow our head
A prayer of thanksgiving for the gift of God's only son
Poured forth from his lips, his words like pearls, every one.
Those precious memories are among my most cherished treasures
Reliving them briefly is one of my life's greatest pleasures

LABOR DAY TO NEW YEAR'S DAY

Oh the good times and celebrations
  From Labor Day with its scorching heat
To New Year's Day with its cold, snow and sleet.

  Labor Day barbecues are so much fun
Underneath September's simmering sun
  A glorious holiday
Chrysanthemums in languorous repose
  Guarding summer's last rose

Days grow shorter and temperature drops
  Farmers gather the pumpkins and apple crops
Autumn is here at last
  The hot summer heat hath passed

October's bright blue weather
  Inspires me to endeavor
To get more exercise
  Regardless of the weather
Jack Frost nibbles at my toes
  And forces me to get out my winter clothes

  Refreshing as the morning dew
Are the radiant leaves in every hue
  Rustling trees of yellow, brown and gold
A magnificent sight to behold

Over the country road to Grandmothers house
  Go every child, grandchild, and spouse
To celebrate Thanksgiving together

The feast is spread
The blessing is said
  With grateful hearts we are over fed

December arrives on a chilly morn
  Announcing the month the Christ child was born
  Happiness, Joy and Emotion
But busy, busy as we rush along
  Shopping and struggling through the throng
Presents for everybody, wrapping and tying bows
  We'll never get it all done, goodness knows.

The Christmas tree stands tall
  Safely secured and tied to the wall
Decorations are neatly placed
  The angel attached and tinsel placed
Presents stacked, a beautiful sight
  Awaiting Christmas night.

Oh the joys of Christmas, seeing family and friends
  Visiting back and forth and parties that never end.
Going to church to raise
  Our voices in thankfulness and praise
The music enthralls our very soul
  Those wonderful carols never get old.

New Year's Day makes its debut, freezing
  And snow clouds teasing
Ending the old year is always sad
  We welcome the New Year
  Get ourselves in gear
And work to get set
  For the greatest year yet.

IN MEMORIAM

Laodecia Dicey Langston, one of our country's most remarkable women.
She loved our nation and risked her life to take her stand
On a cold winter night, a brave girl, just 15,
Walked 20 miles and forded the Tyger stream.
Fell in twice, almost took her life

She walked through the night
Careful to stay out of sight
Determined to warn her brothers of their plight
The Tories planned to raid their camp that night
She warned them in time for them to escape without a fight.

A true Patriot, She performed many daring deeds with determination
To gain victory for a great nation.

The sun was bright in the Piedmont
The day I found her monument
Made of clay and rocks from a chimney of her family's cabin
At last my search had come to an end.

Why had I searched so long to find her resting place?
Because that's where I got my name
Diecy, I'm proud that I can honor her life and fame.

ABOUT THE AUTHOR

Diecy Lawrence Gray Brennemann was born in 1918 and reared in Inman, S.C. She is the mother of four children, grandmother to nine, and great-grandmother to ten. She loves poetry and has written on every subject imaginable. She has been a pioneer for women in the real estate business for over 40 years in Spartanburg, S.C.

To order additional copies of

MY JOURNEY

BY DIECY LAWRENCE

please visit our website at

www.FPSPublishing.com